# CONTENTS

# DEDICATION

*To Kinsley*

# LICENSE

# EASY RUSTIC FRUIT DESSERTS

crostatas, tarts, crumbles, cobblers and more...

Rustic fruit desserts are traditionally known as the seasonal baking of summer fruits in the form of cobblers, crisps, tarts and so much more.

It's a touch of something sweet without too much flour, sugar or heavy dense cake. For those who love fresh fruit desserts this recipe book is for you.

# ABOUT THE AUTHOR & THIS COOKBOOK

I have written this dessert cookbook for those who, like me, love to cook but do not love to bake. There is a saying that "cooks who love to cook do not like to bake and bakers who love to bake do not like to cook". This saying perfectly describes me. However, anyone who loves to cook also wants to, on occasion, serve a lovely dessert that is both delicious and easy to make.

This dessert cookbook is filled with delicious recipes that I hope you will come to love and rely on. You will not need a large Kitchen Aid mixer nor fancy baking tools. I promise that you will come to enjoy the wonderful recipes in this book, many of which can be assembled in 10 minutes or less.

# DESSERTS AND THEIR HISTORY

Starting from the Middle Ages only rich people ate desserts such as preserved fruits or jellies. They were sometimes prepared inside of wafers, which were made from a batter.

Rice pudding was known, but it was not until the 19$^{th}$ century that it was regarded as a medicine. It was often believed to be good for digestive issues.

At Christmas time the Tudors enjoyed mince pies. But at that time they had far more significance than they do now, as the Tudor pies contained thirteen ingredients to represent Jesus and the apostles. Their mince pies also contained currants, prunes, raisins and spices such as cloves, black pepper, mace and saffron. The pies also contained mutton to represent the shepherds.

Cakes were first mentioned as a dessert in 1586.

In the 17$^{th}$ century people in England began to eat ice cream. Over the years trifle came to be, as did creamy mousse recipes.

# HISTORY OF COBBLERS

Cobblers came about in America when the early settlers became expert at improvising. When first arriving to America, the settlers brought with them their favorite recipes such as English pudding. Not able to find many of their native home-based ingredients, American desserts slowly came about.

The early colonists, as a rule, were quite fond of juicy meals made from fruit, whether it was for breakfast, lunch or dinner. It was not until the late 19th century that fruits evolved into desserts, served following a meal.

The history of how Cobblers came to be is strictly American. Cobblers are a deep dish fruit dessert usually topped with a thick crust made from biscuit. The fruit fillings typically are made from seasonal fruits such as peaches, apples or any berries. Some versions of the Cobbler are enclosed in the crust - while others have a drop-biscuit topping.

Crisp and Crumble are different to Cobblers in that the fruit mixture rests on the bottom with a crumb topping. The crumb topping is usually made with some type of flour, oats, cookies or cracker crumb.

A Crumble is the British version of the American Crisp.

A *Crostata* is an Italian baked tart or pie. The earliest known use of a crostata is from a cookbook published in 1465 called "Book of the Art of Cooking". Crostatas are very simple desserts to make. Historically, *Crostata* is defined as "a rustic, free-form version of an open fruit tart".

*Crostatas* are personally my very favorite dessert to prepare.

# QUICK TIPS

For all my recipes I recommend taking note of the following tips.

- o Pie crusts or pie shells.

  I recommend buying good quality frozen pie shells or pie crusts. My favorite brands are Pillsbury, Mrs. Smith and Trader Joe's. If you want to try your hand at making your own pie crust or pie shell, refer to the bonus recipe – Portuguese Almond Tart – for a great pastry dough recipe.

- o Vanilla extract.

  I highly recommend a good quality vanilla extract such as Nielsen-Massey.

- o Butter.

  Recipes which use butter – unsalted butter is recommended.

- o Castor sugar.

  Recipes which call for sugar – castor sugar (also known as superfine sugar) is recommended. Although castor sugar is preferable, using regular white sugar will also work for the dessert.

- o Turbinado sugar.

  Recipes which call for turbinado sugar are best made with this sugar and not any other type of white sugar. 'Sugar In The Raw' is a popular brand of turbinado sugar

- o Confectioner's sugar is the same as powdered sugar.

# RECIPES

# Fig Tart with Sweet Sherry Custard

Many tarts are made using a crust. You can certainly make your own dough for a crust but I find that premade frozen crusts are fabulous and make any dessert so much easier to prepare. I highly recommend using a premade pie shell or crust for this dessert.

## INGREDIENTS

1 frozen tart shell, thawed

12 firm fresh figs

2 large eggs, at room temperature

½ cup sugar

¼ cup all-purpose flour

⅛ cup sweet cream sherry

1 cup heavy cream

1 vanilla bean, sliced in half & seeds scraped out

1 teaspoon vanilla extract

1 fig, sliced for topping

*optional – a pinch of fresh nutmeg or cinnamon*


## DIRECTIONS for the tart shell

Preheat the oven to 375° F.

Thaw the tart shell for approximately 20 minutes at room temperature. I do not recommend using a microwave to defrost.

Prick the bottom and sides of the tart shell with a fork.

Bake the tart shell for approximately 15 minutes, or until golden brown.


## DIRECTIONS for the custard

Reduce oven temperature to 300° F.

Prepare the figs by removing the stems. Wipe them carefully to be sure the skin is clean.

Slice the figs horizontally in half and reserve.

In a medium-sized bowl beat the eggs and sugar until you have a thick, pale yellow-colored mixture.

Slowly add the flour and gently beat until mixed.

Slowly mix in the sherry and heavy cream.

Add the vanilla bean seeds and vanilla extract to the custard.

*Optional* - if using, add the nutmeg or cinnamon.

Use a spatula to gently mix the custard well. Pour the custard into the tart shell.

Arrange the fresh figs on top in a V shape, radiating from the center.

Place the tart shell filled with custard onto a sheet pan and place on the middle rack of the oven. Bake for 30 to 40 minutes.

The edges of the custard should be "set" and the middle of the custard should still be a bit wobbly. The temperature of the custard should be between 170 - 180° F.

Remove from the oven and allow the custard to cool before refrigerating.

Arrange the remaining sliced fig on top for decoration.

# Berry Crostata with Lemon Ricotta Cream

This is one of my favorite desserts. I make crostatas more often than any other dessert and the reason is they are so easy to make and always delicious.

Crostatas are made from pastry dough. If you enjoy making fresh, homemade dough please do so. I am a fan, as mentioned in my introduction, of utilizing the frozen doughs available because the quality for most brands is excellent.

## INGREDIENTS

1 Pillsbury pastry pie crust, thawed

10 oz. fresh blackberries, raspberries or blueberries

16 oz. fresh strawberries, trimmed and cut into quarters

zest of 1 large lemon

pinch of black pepper

*optional – splash of balsamic vinegar for the berries*

*optional – 1 tablespoon flour for the berries*

3 tablespoons blueberry jam (I like Bonne Maman)

1 egg

1 tablespoon turbinado sugar (Sugar In The Raw)

1 tablespoon butter, cut into small pieces

¾ cup heavy cream

¾ cup whole milk ricotta cheese

1 tablespoon honey

*optional – splash of vanilla extract for the ricotta cream*


## DIRECTIONS

Preheat the oven to 400° F.

Place parchment paper onto a sheet pan and unroll the thawed pastry dough out onto it. Do not worry if there are a few rips, just mend by pressing together. Allow the dough to rest while the berries are prepared.

In a large bowl add all the berries. Add the lemon zest, pinch of pepper and (optional) a splash of balsamic vinegar (no more than 1 teaspoon) and stir together with the berries. If you like to add a touch of flour to your pies and crostatas you may do so next. I typically do not add flour, but it is perfectly fine if you do.

Gently spread the blueberry jam onto the pastry dough. It is not necessary to spread the jam edge to edge, just ensure the center part is nicely covered with jam.

Carefully drain the berries of any juice that may have collected and evenly spread the berries over the jam, leaving a 1½-inch border clear on the dough.

Gently fold the edges of the dough up and over the fruit. Tuck and pinch the dough if you like to give it a rustic edge. Mend any rips by simply pinching or folding the dough together.

Beat the egg with a splash of tap water and brush the edges of the dough. It is not necessary to soak the dough with egg, just enough to cover nicely.

Sprinkle the turbinado sugar all over the fruit and the edges of the dough. If you wish you can add a bit more turbinado sugar onto the edges. Finish by dotting the fruit with butter pieces.

Place the sheet pan into the oven and bake for 20 minutes. Turn off the oven and allow the residual heat to finish the crostata, until it is nicely browned. Usually takes another 5 - 7 minutes.

Prepare the ricotta cream by first adding the heavy cream into a chilled bowl. Beat the cream with a mixer until light peaks form.

If you wish, add the vanilla extract next (optional) along with a small amount of lemon zest and honey. Stir into the cream.

Add the ricotta into the cream mixture and beat for 45 seconds.

Chill the ricotta cream before serving together with the crostata.

# Semifreddo with Summer Berries

Semifreddo is an Italian dessert that is a half-frozen cake. It has a mousse-like texture and is very easy to make.

## INGREDIENTS

1 lb. fresh blackberries

½ lb. fresh blueberries

⅓ cup sugar

5 egg yolks

2 whole eggs

2 cups heavy cream, whipped into peaks

½ cup sliced almonds or chopped pistachios

1 tablespoon rosewater

## DIRECTIONS

Line a loaf pan with plastic film (saran wrap), with enough extra to be able to cover over the filling.

In a heatproof bowl add the sugar, egg yolks and whole eggs.

Place the bowl over simmering water in a pot large enough to contain the bowl. Using a hand mixer whisk for 4 - 5 minutes until the mixture is creamy and thick. Remove the bowl from the heat and whisk for another 4 - 5 minutes.

Transfer the mixture into another bowl and fold in the whipped cream, rosewater, nuts and ⅔'s of the berries.

Pour the mixture into the loaf pan. Cover over the top of the filling with the plastic film and refrigerate overnight.

Allow the loaf pan to come to room temperature for 10 minutes before serving.

Slice, plate and garnishing with the remaining ⅓ of fresh berries, and with extra nuts if you wish.

# Mostaccioli Cookie (Roman)

This cookie recipe is a version of one I found that was invented 300 years before the birth of Christ. This specific recipe is from Southern Italy and is a holiday favorite. Rich and very delicious.

## INGREDIENTS

½ cup natural cocoa powder

⅔ cup all-purpose flour

1 teaspoon baking soda

½ cup finely ground almonds or almond meal

¼ cup sugar

1 teaspoon ground cinnamon

pinch of salt

¼ cup honey

¼ cup molasses

¼ water

⅔ cup confectioner's sugar

zest of 1 lemon

juice of 1 lemon

## **<u>DIRECTIONS</u>**

First sift the cocoa powder into a large bowl. Then sift the flour and baking soda into the cocoa powder. Add the ground almonds, sugar, cinnamon and a pinch of salt. Mix to well to incorporate.

Next add the honey, molasses and water. Stir well until the dough gets sticky. Allow any excess liquid to absorb and then chill the cookie dough for 45 - 60 minutes.

Preheat the oven to 325° F.

Place the dough onto a smooth, floured surface and roll it out until it is about ¼-inch thick .

Use a sharp knife to cut the dough into either square or circular shapes. If you have a cookie cutter you can use that as well.

Place the cookie dough onto a cookie sheet pan lined with parchment paper. Dust off any excess flour from the dough before baking. Bake for 15 minutes.

While you allow the cookies to cool slightly - but not fully - prepare the lemon glaze.

To prepare the glaze combine the confectioner's sugar, lemon zest and fresh lemon juice in a bowl. Mix until smooth and then immediately apply onto the slightly warm cookies using either a pastry brush or a spoon.

You can apply a second layer of glaze if you wish.

# Churro Cookie (Italian/Spanish)

A very old cookie recipe. There are many recipes out there on how to make a churro cookie. I use Pillsbury refrigerated or frozen pie crusts. So easy and delicious.

## INGREDIENTS

2 Pillsbury pie crusts, thawed

4 oz. cream cheese, whipped

1 teaspoon vanilla extract

¾ cup sugar

2 tablespoons cinnamon

2 - 3 tablespoons melted butter

## <u>DIRECTIONS</u>

Preheat the oven to 350° F.

In a small bowl combine the cream cheese, vanilla and ¼ of the sugar. Mix and set aside.

Unroll the two pie crusts and spread one of them with the cream cheese mixture.

Place the other pie crust on top of the cream cheese.

Cut the pie crust layers using any size cookie cutter – whatever size you prefer. Crimp the edges of the cookie with a fork to seal the layers.

Place the cookies onto a baking sheet lined with parchment paper and bake for approximately 12 - 13 minutes. They should be golden brown.

Combine the remaining sugar with the cinnamon and mix to make cinnamon sugar.

Allow the cookies to cool slightly and then brush the tops with melted butter. Finish the cookies with a sprinkle of cinnamon sugar, as much or as little cinnamon sugar as you like.

# Italian Strawberry Mousse

A delicious and refreshing summer dessert that is finished with a touch of balsamic vinegar.

## INGREDIENTS

1 lb. strawberries

3 oz. confectioner's sugar

12 fresh mint leaves

1 oz. gelatin sheets

1 ½ cups heavy cream, whipped

splash of balsamic vinegar glaze

## **DIRECTIONS**

Clean and slice the strawberries. Place the strawberries and confectioner's sugar in a blender and mix until they become a puree.

Prepare the gelatin by placing the sheets in a bowl of warm water. You need 1.3 lbs. (about 2 ½ cups) of warm water for every 1 oz. of gelatin.

As the gelatin soaks heat a ⅓ of the prepared strawberry puree in a sauce pan on medium heat. When the puree begins to simmer add the gelatin. Be sure the gelatin has completely dissolved before adding the remaining strawberry puree.

Cool the strawberry mixture.

Whisk your whipped cream until it has formed nice peaks. Carefully fold it into the cooled strawberry puree.

Pour the strawberry mousse into small serving cups. Cover and refrigerate for 24 hours.

To serve, turn the cups over onto a serving plate. Add fresh strawberries and mint to decorate.

Optional - Decorate by mixing 1 tablespoon warmed strawberry jam with 1 teaspoon balsamic vinegar glaze. Spread a thin decorative layer on the top and the side of the plate. If desired set on a thin cookie wafer.

# Twister Cake

A classically American cake that was developed years ago in Texas. It is an easy cake to prepare that's made with canned or fresh fruit, coconut and brown sugar.

## INGREDIENTS

For the Cake

2 cups all-purpose flour

2 teaspoon baking soda

2 extra large eggs

1 ½ cups white sugar

2 cups canned fruit (drained) or you can use fresh peaches, pineapple or soft pears

¼ cup light brown sugar

1 cup chopped walnuts

For the Icing

1 stick unsalted butter

1 cup sweet flaked coconut

⅔ cup light brown sugar

½ cup evaporated milk

*optional – splash of vanilla extract*

## DIRECTIONS

Preheat the oven to 325° F.

Butter a 9 x 13-inch baking dish.

For the cake:

To a medium-sized bowl add the flour, baking soda, eggs, white sugar and fruit. Using a hand mixer on very low speed blend until just combined. Use a spatula to scrape the bottom of the bowl and mix well to incorporate.

Pour the batter into the buttered baking dish, making sure the batter is level and evenly spread.

In a small bowl combine the brown sugar and nuts. Sprinkle evenly over the batter.

Bake in the oven for 40 - 45 minutes, or until the cake is done – firm to the touch in the middle.

For the icing:

While the cake is baking prepare the icing by combining the butter, coconut, brown sugar and the evaporated milk in a saucepan. Optional -add a splash of vanilla extract. Heat the saucepan on medium heat until the icing mixture begins to boil. Turn the heat to low and simmer for 3 - 4 minutes, or until the cake is done.

Remove the cake from the oven when done and immediately pour the icing over the top of the cake, while the icing and the cake are still hot.

Cool the cake for 1 hour before serving.

# Pumpkin Cake

I like cakes that are very easy to make from prepared cake mixes. This is a very good recipe that I discovered many years ago that I hope will become a favorite in your house during the fall and winter months.

## INGREDIENTS

1 yellow cake mix, Duncan Hines

¾ cup unsalted butter (1 ½ sticks)

4 extra large eggs at room temperature

1 can (29 oz.) plain pumpkin puree (not pie filling)

2 teaspoons cinnamon

½ teaspoon ground cloves (you can use less if you wish)

1 teaspoon ground ginger

½ cup light brown sugar

1 cup white sugar

⅔ cup whole milk

1 cup chopped pecan nuts or walnuts

## **DIRECTIONS**

Preheat the oven to 350° F.

Butter a 9 x 13-inch baking dish.

Reserve 1 cup of the cake mix in a bowl. In another bowl combine the remaining cake mix, 1 egg and 1 stick of butter. Mix well using a hand mixer and then pour the batter into the baking dish.

In a clean bowl combine the pumpkin puree, 3 eggs, the cinnamon, cloves, ginger, brown sugar, ½ a cup of white sugar and the milk. Mix well using a hand mixer and then pour in an even layer over the cake batter.

Finally, mix together the reserved 1 cup of cake mix with ½ a stick of butter, ½ a cup white sugar and the nuts. Sprinkle over the top of the pumpkin batter.

Place the baking dish into the oven and bake for 55 - 60 minutes. Test for doneness. If needed, you may finish the cake by turning off the oven and allowing the cake to finish baking using the residual heat of the oven - another 10 minutes.

Allow the cake to cool and then serve.

Optional - decorate cake with nuts and warm caramel sauce.

# BLUEBERRIES & HEAVY CREAM
## TOPPED WITH BROWN SUGAR

One of the simplest desserts you will ever make and is so delicious. This is a real winner for anyone who does not like rich desserts but sometimes wants a slightly sweet and easy to digest dessert.

## **INGREDIENTS**

½ cup fresh blueberries

2 - 4 tablespoons heavy cream

1 teaspoon brown sugar

*optional – sprig of fresh mint*

<u>**DIRECTIONS**</u>

Assemble the dessert by placing the fresh blueberries in a decorative bowl and topping with 2 to 4 tablespoons of heavy cream. Finish by sprinkling the top with brown sugar.

If you wish you can serve with a sprig of fresh mint.

# BALSAMIC BERRIES WITH SCHLAG (SOFT WHIPPED CREAM)

This is a recipe I learnt years ago when working in a gourmet country restaurant. I used to make this very often for my kids when they were still living at home. It's a winner for any time of year.

## INGREDIENTS

5 cups of berries (choice of strawberries, blueberries, blackberries and raspberries)

4 tablespoons balsamic vinegar

½ pint heavy cream

splash of vanilla extract

*optional – splash of Grand Marnier orange liqueur*

# <u>DIRECTIONS</u>

Clean and halve the strawberries if using.

In a medium-sized bowl combine the fresh berries of your choosing and pour over the balsamic vinegar. Gently stir to coat the berries with the balsamic vinegar, being careful not to bruise the berries.

Cover the bowl with plastic wrap (saran) and allow the berries to rest in the refrigerator overnight or for at least 5 hours.

Serve with *schlag* (whipped cream).

To prepare the whipped cream – combine the heavy cream with a splash of vanilla extract and (optional) Grand Marnier. Whip until you just have soft peaks.

# SUMMER DESSERT PIZZA

Your kids will love this summer-time fruit pizza.

## INGREDIENTS

1 Pillsbury pie crust, thawed

4 oz. whipped cream cheese, at room temperature

¼ cup confectioner's sugar

1 cup heavy cream, whipped until peaks form

1 cup fresh strawberries, cleaned and sliced

2 kiwifruits, peeled and sliced

⅓ cup fresh blueberries

⅓ cup fresh blackberries

For the Glaze

¼ cup sugar

2 teaspoon cornstarch

¼ cup fresh orange juice

¼ cup water

zest of 1 orange

## DIRECTIONS

Preheat the oven to 350° F.

Cover a sheet pan with parchment paper. Unroll the thawed dough onto parchment paper. Bake for 14 - 15 minutes.

Cool for 30 minutes.

Once you have the pie crust cooling prepare the glaze for the pizza topping. Combine in a small saucepan the white sugar and cornstarch. Place the pot on medium heat and slowly add the water and orange juice until the mixture comes to a light boil. Stir and simmer for 2 - 3 minutes. Cool the glaze mixture for 30 minutes.

For the cream cheese topping – combine in a small bowl the cream cheese and the confectioner's sugar. Using a hand mixer beat until combined and smooth. Add the freshly whipped heavy cream and stir. Spread over the cooled crust.

Arrange the fresh fruit over the cream cheese mixture just before you are ready to glaze the fruit.

Drizzle the cooled glaze over the fruit.

Refrigerate for 30 minutes and then serve.

# Blueberry Slump in a Skillet

Slump – such a funny name. What is it? It is a classic New England dessert that according to the James Beard Foundation is "a cobbler or grunt style dessert made with fresh fruit that is cooked until thick, then topped with dollops of dough and baked". It can be made with any fruit although blueberries are the most traditional.

Here is how to make one. For this recipe you can use a cast iron skillet, which is traditional in New England, or a baking dish.

## INGREDIENTS for the blueberry mixture

1 quart fresh blueberries

1 ½ cups white sugar

½ teaspoon freshly ground nutmeg

½ cup tap water

splash of vanilla extract

splash of fresh orange juice

zest of one small lemon


## INGREDIENTS for the dumpling mixture

1 cup flour

1 teaspoon baking soda

pinch of salt

1 tablespoon sugar

1 egg, lightly beaten

3 tablespoons whole milk

1 tablespoon butter, melted


## DIRECTIONS

Preheat the oven to 400° F.

*Quick tip* - If using a cast iron skillet, you can prepare the blueberry mixture by adding the ingredients right into the skillet pan (as described in the next paragraph). Proceed by adding the dumplings into the blueberry mixture and baking in the oven. If you use a baking dish prepare the blueberries in a medium-sized saucepan first and then pour the hot mixture into the baking dish.


To prepare the blueberry mixture - place the blueberries, 1 ½ cups sugar, nutmeg and water into the cast iron skillet on medium heat and cook until the blueberries breakdown. You will want to stir a few times so the blueberries do not stick to the bottom of the pan. When the blueberries are cooked down add a splash of vanilla extract, the orange juice and lemon zest. Cook for 1 minute and then turn the heat off.

To prepare the dumplings – into a medium-sized bowl sift the flour, baking soda, pinch of salt and 1 tablespoon of sugar. Set aside.

In another bowl combine the egg, milk and melted butter. Add the dry flour mixture. Blend using a whisk, or hand mixer, until well incorporated.


To prepare the Slump - drop the dumpling dough by the spoonful onto the blueberry mixture. You should get 6 dumplings. Cover the skillet, or baking dish, with foil and bake for 10 minutes.

Uncover the baking dish and serve the individual portions. Top with some blueberries if you wish.

Serve with whipped fresh heavy cream or ice cream.

# PEACH MELBA WITH RASPBERRY PUREE

Peach Melba has become an American Favorite. It is a dessert that was invented in 1892 by the French chef Auguste Escoffier at the Savoy Hotel in London. He made this dessert to honor the Australian soprano Nellie Melba.

## INGREDIENTS

5 peaches, ripe but firm

1 cup regular white sugar

1 vanilla bean, split & seeds removed

7 oz. fresh raspberries

zest of ½ a lemon

½ cup confectioner's sugar

3 oz. sliced almonds

1 ½ cup heavy cream, whipped to firm peaks

*optional – vanilla ice cream*


## **DIRECTIONS**

Bring 2 cups of water to a boil in a medium-sized saucepan.

Dip the peaches into the boiling water for 4 minutes.

Remove the peaches from the boiling water and allow them to cool for a few minutes before peeling. Cut the peaches in half and remove the pit.

Discard the water from the saucepan used for the peaches and add a fresh quart of water. Add the regular white sugar and vanilla seeds (you can also include the vanilla pod for extra flavor). Bring the water mixture to a boil.

Add the peach halves to a colander and dip the peaches into the boiling water mixture for approximately 8 minutes, or until the peaches are soft and can be easily pierced with a knife.

Set the colander aside and allow the peaches to cool.

For the raspberry icing – add the raspberries, lemon zest and confectioner's sugar to a saucepan. Heat on medium-low heat, stirring well, until the raspberries become like a puree.

To serve add the peaches into a decorative bowl and top with whipped cream and (optional) ice cream. Finish with a sprinkle of sliced almonds and a drizzle of the raspberry puree.

# Mixed Berries in Grand Marnier

This is a recipe I used to make for large catering events. It is a wonderful option to a trifle that you might make on special occasions.


## INGREDIENTS

10 cups of blueberries, raspberries, blackberries, strawberries and kiwi

½ - 1 cup Grand Marnier orange liqueur

*optional – whipped heavy cream*

<u>**DIRECTIONS**</u>

Add the all the berries into a large bowl along with the Grand Marnier. Gently stir to coat the berries with Grand Marnier, being careful not to bruise the berries.

Cover the bowl with plastic wrap and leave the berries to marinate for 2 - 6 hours.

*Quick tip* - Slice the strawberries and kiwi in half. You can substitute more of one fruit and less of another, as you prefer.

*Optional – serve with heavy cream whipped into soft peaks.*

# Apple Cream Cheese Crostata

Apple and cream cheese works so well together in this recipe. If you love cheesecake but want something fast you will love this recipe.

## INGREDIENTS

1 Pillsbury pie crust, thawed

4 - 5 apples, peeled and cored and sliced into wedges

2 tablespoons turbinado sugar (Sugar In The Raw)

½ teaspoon cinnamon

¼ teaspoon nutmeg

pinch of black pepper

*optional – 1 teaspoon of sugared ginger, cut into thin slices*

<u>**INGREDIENTS for the Cream Cheese filling**</u>

4 oz. whipped cream cheese

1 tablespoon white sugar

1 teaspoon vanilla extract


<u>**DIRECTIONS**</u>

Preheat the oven to 400° F

Add the apples, turbinado sugar, cinnamon, nutmeg, black pepper and (optional) sugared ginger in a large bowl. Mix to combine.

Add the cream cheese, sugar and vanilla extract to a small bowl and stir gently to combine.

Cover a sheet pan with parchment paper. Unroll the pie crust on top. Trim off any overhang.

Spread the cream cheese over the pie crust, leaving an uncovered border of 1 ½ inches.

Pour the apple mixture in the center of the cream cheese and spread evenly.

Pull the edges of the pie crust up and fold over, pinching to mold rough edges.

You can do an egg wash (egg beaten with a splash of water) or a light brushing of milk over the crust.

Finish by sprinkling a little turbinado sugar all over the top.

Bake for 20 - 25 minutes, or until the crust is nicely browned.

# PEACH CRISP WITH GRANOLA AND YOGURT

This is a wonderful recipe that makes a great dessert or a healthy breakfast.

## **INGREDIENTS**

8 firm peaches, peeled, pit removed and cut into slices

2 tablespoons fresh lemon juice

1 ½ tablespoons arrowroot powder

3 - 4 tablespoons light brown sugar

1 teaspoon vanilla extract

pinch of ground ginger

2 cups prepared granola

1 tablespoon extra virgin olive oil

3 tablespoons vanilla Greek yogurt (per serving)

Bakeware needed – 8-inch pie pan, greased

## DIRECTIONS

Preheat the oven to 375° F.

In a large bowl combine the lemon juice and arrowroot and whisk to form slurry. Stir in the brown sugar, vanilla extract and ground ginger.

Add the peaches and mix well to coat.

Pour the peaches into the prepared pie pan. Bake the peaches until they are starting to soften, approximately 10 minutes

While the peaches are cooking combine the granola with the olive oil.

After 10 minutes remove the pie pan from the oven and top the peaches with the granola/olive oil mixture. Lightly press the granola into the peaches.

Place the pie pan back into the oven and reduce the oven temperature to 350° F. The crisp will be done in 10 - 15 minutes.

Serve the crisp warm topped with Greek yogurt.

# Strawberry Shortcake

For this recipe you can buy from your local grocer their bakery biscuits, lemon cake, sponge cake or shortcake cups.

## INGREDIENTS

1 quart fresh strawberries

splash of balsamic vinegar

¼ cup regular white sugar

pinch of black pepper

1 cup heavy cream, whipped into soft peaks

pinch of sugar

1 teaspoon vanilla extract

*optional – sliced strawberries for topping*

<u>**DIRECTIONS**</u>

Combine the strawberries, balsamic vinegar, sugar and a pinch of black pepper in a large bowl. Stir to mix. Cover with plastic wrap and chill for one hour in the refrigerator.

To serve - plate your selected base (biscuit, lemon cake or shortcake cups) and, using a slotted spoon, smother the base with the strawberry mixture. If you wish to build a second layer, repeat with another layer of base and strawberry mixture.

Top each serving with a dollop of freshly whipped cream.

*Optional – top the cream with a few slices of strawberry.*

# TARTE TATIN IN RICH YOGURT CREAM

Apples are wonderful to use for this dessert but you can also substitute with pears. This recipe includes cranberries which add a delicate tartness that balances well with the rich yogurt cream.

## INGREDIENTS

1 Pillsbury pie crust, thawed or refrigerated

2 tablespoons butter

½ cup sugar

5 Pink Lady or Red Delicious apples, sliced into wedges

¾ cup cranberries

½ cup heavy cream

½ cup plain Greek yogurt

## DIRECTIONS

Preheat the oven to 425° F.

*Quick tip* – A cast iron skillet is best for this dish.

Place the butter and sugar into a 9-inch cast iron skillet, or an ovenproof skillet, on medium heat. Heat until the mixture reaches a caramel color, approximately 4 minutes. Stir every minute.

Remove the skillet from the stove and add the apple wedges in a decorative pattern on the caramel inside the skillet. After all the apples are arranged sprinkle the cranberries over the apples.

Bake for 25 minutes.

Remove from the oven and allow the pan to cool for 30 minutes.

Unroll the pie crust onto an ungreased baking sheet. Prick the pie crust all over with a fork and then bake in the oven for 8 - 10 minutes.

While the pie crust is baking add the heavy cream to a small bowl and using a hand mixer beat until peaks form. Gently fold the whipped cream into the yogurt. Chill in the refrigerator.

When ready to make the tartin – gently place the pastry over the apples which are in the skillet. Place a serving plate over the top of the pastry and trim the edges of excess pastry. The plate should just fit inside the top of the skillet.

When ready to invert – hold the skillet firmly by the handle and place your other hand firmly on the plate. In one movement flip the skillet over (be sure to keep your hand pressing firmly on the plate) and then place the plate onto the counter. Gently lift the skillet from the apples. Should any apples stick to the pan either discard or add back to the pie.

Serve warm with the yogurt cream.

# PECAN PIE WITH CRANBERRIES

This recipe will make a lovely deep dish pie without a top layer.

## INGREDIENTS

1 Pillsbury pie crust, thawed or refrigerated

1 ½ teaspoons vanilla extract

⅓ cup butter, melted

3 extra large eggs

1 cup light corn syrup

*optional – splash of bourbon (no more than ½ tablespoon)*

2 cups cranberries

1 ½ cups chopped pecans

*Quick tip* – multiply all ingredients x 1.5 for a deep dish pie.

<u>**DIRECTIONS**</u>

Preheat the oven to 425° F.

Unroll the pie crust and place into your selected pie pan. Crimp the edges with a fork.

In a large bowl whisk all of the ingredients listed above except the cranberries and pecans. When fully incorporated stir in the cranberries and pecans.

Pour the mixture into the pie crust.

For the best results bake on the lowest rack in your oven for 10 minutes. Reduce the heat to 350° F and bake for a further 40 minutes. If you are baking a deep dish pie, bake for 50 minutes.

Cool for 30 minutes before serving.

# Easy Jam Tart

For many people making tarts can be intimidating. I searched for how to make a tart that was easy and stress free and found that, as with crostata, tarts can also be quite easily made. The wonderful thing about this jam tart is that you can make it at any time of year with any kind of jam you like. I would not recommend using a jelly for this tart as it's too runny.

## INGREDIENTS

2 Pillsbury pie crusts, thawed

2 cups jam (apricot, blueberry, raspberry, marmalade, mixed berry or fig), I recommend Bonne Maman

pinch of salt

¼ cup turbinado sugar (Sugar In The Raw)

1 egg, beaten

## DIRECTIONS

Preheat the oven to 350° F.

Lay one of the thawed pie crusts into a tart pan or a springform pan. Press the pie crust gently into the sides and gently fork the bottom of the crust.

Add the jam onto the crust and evenly spread to cover the entire pie crust.

Take the other pie crust and lay it fully on top, or you can slice long strips and cover the jam in a decorative fashion.

When you are happy with how the top layer looks, gently brush the strips or the top crust with beaten egg. Sprinkle the turbinado sugar all over the top.

Place the tart into the oven and bake for approximately 20 - 25 minutes, or until the crust has a nice brown color.

Remove the tart and cool for 10 minutes before serving.

Serve at room temperature with or without whipped cream or ice cream.

# STRAWBERRIES IN WHITE WINE

This is the easiest dessert in the world to make and very elegant.

## <u>INGREDIENTS</u>

5 cups fresh strawberries

1 cup sugar

splash of balsamic vinegar

2 cups dry white wine, preferably Sauvignon Blanc

1 bunch of fresh mint

fresh mint leaves for topping

# **DIRECTIONS**

Cut the strawberries in half. Place the cut strawberries into a large bowl and sprinkle with sugar.

Add the balsamic vinegar and white wine and stir. Scatter the bunch of mint over the strawberries and stir.

Cover the bowl with plastic wrap (saran) and chill for 1 hour in the fridge.

After 1 hour uncover the bowl and give the strawberries a stir. Cover the bowl again and chill for another 1 hour.

To serve stir the strawberries well and remove the mint. Discard the mint.

Place the strawberries and the white wine liquid into serving glasses.

Top each serving with one or two mint leaves.

# Caramelized Sweet Peaches

So simple and so delicious. If you love summer peaches please try this easy recipe. You will make it over and over again.

## INGREDIENTS

5 fresh peaches, cut in half and pits removed

zest of 1 lemon

juice of 1 lemon

pinch of salt

pinch of cinnamon

½ stick unsalted butter

¼ cup light brown sugar

2 tablespoons dark rum or cognac

*optional – whipped heavy cream or ice cream*

<u>**DIRECTIONS**</u>

Slice the peaches into thick wedges or leave in half.

To a medium-sized bowl add the peach wedges or halves, the lemon zest and juice, pinch of salt and pinch of cinnamon. Stir and set aside for 20 minutes.

After the peaches have rested melt the butter and light brown sugar in a skillet over medium heat. Add the peaches and the liquid into the pan and gently cook for approximately 5 - 7 minutes, or until caramelized. Add the dark rum or cognac and simmer for 1 minute. Turn the heat off.

Allow the peaches to cool for 5 minutes before serving with whipped cream or ice cream.

# BAKED PLUM PIE WITH MASCARPONE CREAM

Plums are considered a stone fruit in Europe and are beloved by many countries. They bake beautifully and with a little sugar added they make a wonderful, easy and rustic-style fruit dessert.

I recommend preparing this pie one full day ahead as all the ingredients need to be properly chilled.

This is a beautiful pie for any special occasion.

## INGREDIENTS

1 premade pie crust, thawed

3 - 4 lbs. fresh ripe plums, cut in half & pits removed

1 ½ cups regular white sugar

zest of 1 lemon

2 tablespoons fresh lemon juice

1 tablespoon vanilla extract

pinch of freshly cracked black pepper

2 tablespoons confectioner's sugar

8 oz. mascarpone cheese

⅓ cup crème fraiche

whipped heavy cream

## **DIRECTIONS**

Preheat the oven to 350° F.

Bake the pie crust according to the box instructions.

To a large bowl add the plums, white sugar, lemon zest, lemon juice, vanilla extract and black pepper and stir.

Divide the plums between two baking dishes.

Place the baking dishes into the oven and roast the plums for approximately 40 minutes, or until the plums are bubbling and tender but not falling apart. You can continue baking for a further 10 minutes if needed.

Remove the baking dishes from the oven and allow the plums to cool.

Once the plums are cooled remove them from the baking dishes and place them onto a platter. Cover the platter with plastic wrap and chill in the refrigerator.

Pour the remaining juices from the baking dishes into a saucepan. Bring the juices to a boil until thickened into a glaze. Allow to cool and then chill in the refrigerator.

Add 2 tablespoons of confectioner's sugar, the mascarpone and crème fraiche to a bowl.

Using a hand mixer beat until nice peaks form, but do not over mix.

Chill the mixture in the refrigerator along with the plums and the glaze.

When ready to prepare the pie remove all the items from the refrigerator.

Spread the mascarpone cream mixture evenly on the pie crust.

Arrange the chilled plums in a tight circular layer (without overlapping).

Once the first layer is arranged begin to arrange the second layer, overlapping until a tight spiral is made. The plums can form a dome in the center.

Use a pastry brush to spread the plum glaze over the plums. If the glaze is too thick and hard you can gently reheat with 1 tablespoon of water.

To serve the pie - cut into slices and top with freshly made whipped cream.

*Quick tip* – finish with fresh mint leaves for a beautiful presentation.

# BAKED APPLE ROSES

A stunningly beautiful dessert that might look difficult to make but is actually very easy. This recipe is made using frozen puff pastry dough. It takes about 20 minutes to prepare.

## INGREDIENTS

1 puff pastry sheet, thawed

2 red apples, red delicious or honey crisp

2 tablespoons fresh lemon juice

zest of ½ lemon

3 tablespoons apricot or fig jam (I recommend Bonne Maman)

1 tablespoon confectioner's sugar for topping

*optional – freshly ground cinnamon*

Bakeware needed – muffin pans (buttered and floured) or a silicone muffin pan.

## **DIRECTIONS**

Preheat the oven to 375° F.

Begin by microwaving the apples to soften them - the method of preparation follows.

First add the water and lemon juice into a microwavable bowl.

Cut the unpeeled apples in half and remove the core. Wash the apples to be certain they are very clean. Then slice the apple halves into very thin slices.

Place the apples slices into the lemon water and microwave for 3 minutes. Test one of the apple slices to be sure it is soft enough so it will not break when bent slightly. If it does break you need to microwave the apple slices for another 30 seconds.

On a floured counter unwrap the puff pastry. Use a rolling pin to stretch the puff pastry into a rectangular shape large enough so that you can cut 6 strips of about 2 x 9 inches.

In a bowl combine the apricot or fig jam with 2 tablespoons of warm tap water. Stir to mix until a nice smooth paste is formed. If needed you can microwave for 30 seconds to soften the mixture more.

Next drain the apples.

Coat each puff pastry piece with a thin layer of jam.

If needed pat dry the apples slices and place the slices in an overlap onto each puff pastry piece. Be sure the skin side of the apple is on the outside and not covered.

*Optional* - sprinkle cinnamon onto the apples.

Method of forming the roses:

* Carefully fold up the bottom part of the pastry;
* Starting at one end gently roll the pastry, being careful to keep the apple slices in place.
* Seal the edges at the end by pressing lightly with your fingers;
* Gently place the apple pastry roll into one of the muffin cups;
* Repeat until all of the pastry strips are used.


Bake at 375° F for 40 - 45 minutes on the lowest oven rack. After 25 minutes check to be certain the pastry is not burning.

Remove from oven and cool slightly before serving.

Sprinkle lightly with confectioner's sugar.

*Quick tip* – for the best results, serve the baked roses within an hour.

# BLUEBERRY CRISP

So easy to make and so delicious. Blueberry Crisp is the perfect dessert for busy moms and those who just want something quick and easy to make for a dinner party or for a weeknight after-dinner dessert.

*Quick tip* – many crisp recipes call for a heavy, thick crisp crust. This recipe is quite different. It is a light dusting of crisp over delicious fresh blueberries, baked until just done.

## INGREDIENTS

1 pint fresh blueberries

zest of 1 lemon

pinch of freshly cracked black pepper

splash of balsamic vinegar

pinch of turbinado sugar (Sugar In The Raw)

1 teaspoon vanilla extract

butter for greasing the baking dish

## INGREDIENTS for the Crisp

2 tablespoons melted butter

½ cup quick oats

1 teaspoon all-purpose flour

2 tablespoons light brown sugar

pinch of salt

pinch of cinnamon

*optional – small handful of toasted finely chopped almonds, walnuts or pecans*


## DIRECTIONS

Preheat the oven to 375° F.

Combine all the blueberry ingredients in a small bowl.

Lightly butter a small, shallow baking dish.

Pour the blueberries into the baking dish.

Prepare the crisp topping by adding the oatmeal, flour, light brown sugar, melted butter, salt, cinnamon and nuts (if using). Stir well with your fingers, or use a fork to mix, until fully incorporated.

Sprinkle the crisp mixture all over the top in a thin layer. It is not necessary to cover end to end.

Place the baking dish into the oven and bake for 20 - 30 minutes, or until the blueberries are bubbly and the crisp topping is nicely browned.

# Strawberry Ricotta Tart

I recommend buying a premade graham cracker crumb pie crust for this elegant, but ever so easy, tart recipe.

## INGREDIENTS

1 premade graham cracker crumb pie crust

8 oz. whole milk ricotta cheese

1 ½ tablespoons sugar

zest of 1 orange

1 ½ lb. fresh strawberries, hulled & halved

3 tablespoons strawberry or red currant jam

1 tablespoon Grand Marnier or fresh orange juice

<u>**DIRECTIONS**</u>

Whisk the ricotta, sugar and the orange zest together until incorporated.

Spread the ricotta mixture over the graham cracker crust.

Place the strawberries in a decorative circular pattern on top of the ricotta.

Combine the jam and the Grand Marnier in a small saucepan and bring to a gentle simmer. Mix well to incorporate. Remove from heat as soon as the jam is warm.

Allow the jam to cool.

When the jam is cool, but still runny, use a basting brush to coat the strawberries.

Refrigerate the tart for one hour before serving. It is okay to leave it uncovered.

*Quick tip* – most tarts with fresh berries need to be eaten within a few hours or else the juices from the fruit will be released and make the crust soggy.

# WINTER PIE

A delicious pie made from fruit that is traditionally stored for the winter months. Apples and pears primarily.

## INGREDIENTS

2 thawed pie crusts (I like Pillsbury pie crusts/rolls)

3 cups apples sliced into ½" slices (any kind of baking apple you prefer)

3 cups pears sliced into ½" slices

1 cup cranberries

1 cup raisins

pinch of black pepper

pinch of nutmeg

1 teaspoon vanilla extract

2 tablespoons corn starch

½  cup light brown sugar

1 tablespoon butter

*optional – egg wash (1 egg beaten with a teaspoon of water)*

## DIRECTIONS

Preheat the oven to 425° F.

Thaw the pie crusts.

In a large bowl combine the apples, pears, cranberries, raisins, black pepper, nutmeg and the vanilla extract. Stir well to mix.

Add the cornstarch and light brown sugar. Mix well.

Mold one of the pie crusts into a pie pan.

Pour the fruit mixture into the center of pie pan to form a mound in the center, keeping the edges clear.

Dot the butter all over the top of the fruit.

Lay the other pie crust over the fruit and crimp the edges with a fork to seal. Make a few decorative slits in the top of the crust.

If you wish you can lightly brush the pie crust with an egg wash.

Place into the oven and bake for 45 - 50 minutes.

Allow to cool for 15 minutes before serving.

# PEAR SAUCE FOR ICE CREAM

The first time I tried to make pear sauce for ice cream I made the mistake of not allowing the pears to marinate overnight. This is a crucial step that I recommend you do not skip. Otherwise, it's a very easy sauce to make for ice cream, or even a pound cake or white cake.

## INGREDIENTS

6 - 7 Bartlett pears, peeled (be sure they are ripe)

½ cup sugar

1 small lemon, peeled and segmented

1 small orange, peeled and segmented

¾ cup chopped walnuts

½ cup golden raisins

pinch of cinnamon

## DIRECTIONS

Combine the pears and sugar in a plastic bag . Give the bag a good shake before laying the bag flat on a plate and refrigerating overnight.

*Quick tip* – be sure to peel the lemon and orange. Just use the fruit segments for this dish.

When ready to make the sauce, add the lemon segments, orange segments, walnuts, raisins and cinnamon into a saucepan.

Add the pears, with all their liquid, to the pan.

Cover the pan and cook for 30 minutes on medium heat, or until the pear mixture is soft and a thick sauce has formed. Give it a good stir.

Allow the sauce to cool slightly.

Serve over ice cream or pound cake.

# Rum & Raisin Rice Pudding

Absolutely delicious. If you have family members who love rice pudding they will love this recipe.

## INGREDIENTS

2 ½ tablespoons Meyers Dark Rum

¾ cup raisins

drizzle of olive oil

1 cup basmati rice

pinch of salt

1 ¾ cups tap water

6 cups half-and-half (or 3 cups heavy cream & 3 cups whole milk)

½ cup sugar

2 teaspoons vanilla extract

1 egg, beaten

<u>**DIRECTIONS**</u>

Add the rum and raisins to a bowl and allow the raisins to absorb the rum while you make the rice.

To a large pot on medium heat add a small amount of olive oil. When the oil is hot add the rice and a pinch of salt. Stir the rice to coat with the olive oil. After 2 minutes add the tap water.

Bring the rice to a boil. Reduce heat to a simmer and cover tightly with a lid.

After 10 minutes remove the lid and add 5 cups of the half-and-half along with the sugar and vanilla extract. Bring to a boil and then reduce the heat to a simmer, leaving the pot uncovered.

After 7 minutes slowly stir the rice mixture and continue cooking for another 8 minutes. After the 15 minutes have passed begin to slowly stir the rice for another 10 minutes.

Slowly add the beaten egg into the rice. Stir for one full minute and then remove the saucepan from the heat.

Add the raisins and the rum and stir in the remaining cup of half-and-half.

Pour the hot mixture into a bowl and allow the pudding to cool for 10 minutes.

Cover the bowl with plastic film, pushing the film down onto the top of the pudding to prevent a crust from forming.

Refrigerate for several hours.

*Quick tip* – you can serve this rice pudding gently warmed (but not hot) or serve it at room temperature.

# APPLE CRISP WITH BRANDY soaked GOLDEN RAISINS

There are so many different varieties of apples here in the US. The colonists planted over 150 different varieties of apple trees just in New England. Apples are often used in a double crust pie such the my Winter Pie. However, they are also fantastic as a crisp.

## INGREDIENTS for the Filling

4 lbs. Granny Smith apples, peeled, cored and sliced

1 ½ cups golden raisins

4 tablespoons cognac or good brandy

⅓ cup sugar

1 level teaspoon cinnamon

pinch of nutmeg

pinch of black pepper

1 tablespoon all-purpose flour

1 tablespoon fresh lemon juice

zest of 1 lemon

## **INGREDIENTS for the crisp topping**

1 cup quick oats

¾ cup light brown sugar

⅔ cup all-purpose flour

pinch of salt

½ teaspoon cinnamon

1 ½ sticks unsalted butter, softened

½ cup chopped walnuts

## **DIRECTIONS**

Preheat the oven to 375° F.

Combine the raisins and the cognac or brandy in a bowl and allow the raisins to soak for 30 minutes. Then drain the raisins.

Mix the oats, light brown sugar, flour, salt and cinnamon together in a bowl. Add the softened butter and mix together with a fork. Once you have large chunks mix in the walnuts.

Combine the apples, raisins, sugar, cinnamon, nutmeg, black pepper, flour, lemon juice and lemon zest in a bowl and mix well.

Pour the apples into a baking dish which has been lightly greased with a small amount of butter.

Sprinkle the crisp topping all over the apples. Do not heavily coat the apples with crisp.

Bake for 45 - 50 minutes, or until the apple mixture is bubbly and the crisp topping is nicely browned.

Optional - if desired replace crisp with a thin layer of phyllo.

# Strawberry Zabaglione with Marsala

Strawberry Zabaglione is very easy to make and is a perfect dessert on a date night.

## INGREDIENTS

8 - 10 fresh strawberries, cleaned and slice into small wedges

2 tablespoons sugar

## INGREDIENTS for the Zabaglione

3 egg yolks

2 oz. Marsala wine

2 tablespoons sugar

## DIRECTIONS

Combine the strawberries and sugar in a bowl and cover the bowl with plastic wrap. Marinate for 1 - 2 hours. No longer or the strawberries will get too soupy.

Place the strawberries into dessert glasses.

Then prepare the Zabaglione.

Combine all of the ingredients in a glass bowl and whisk by hand for several minutes.

Then place the bowl over a pot of boiling water. Whisk briskly and continuously until the egg mixture begins to form a foamy custard-like texture. This will take 6 - 7 minutes.

Test the custard by pulling up the whisk. You should have a nice smooth and creamy custard foam.

Top the strawberries with the warm custard.

*Quick tip* – finish by topping the Zabaglione with a light covering of shaved dark chocolate.

# ITALIAN ZABAGLIONE WITH LIMONCELLO

## INGREDIENTS

5 egg yolks

2 tablespoons sugar

2 oz. Limoncello liqueur

zest of 1 small lemon

*optional – serve with biscotti or over raspberries*

## DIRECTIONS

Prepare a pot of boiling water.

Whisk together the egg yolks and sugar until the egg yolks are broken and the sugar has dissolved.

Next add the limoncello. Whisk briskly until the egg yolks begin to get fluffy and a custard develops.

Place the bowl over the boiling water. Continue to whisk until the custard develops a creamy yellow color. Taste to see if more Limoncello liqueur is needed.

Pour the custard into serving glasses and sprinkle with lemon zest.

# Fruit Clafoutis

Clafoutis is a French dessert that is traditionally made with cherries but any ripe, tender fruit will work.

It is an elegant dessert that is very easy to make.

You can use your blender to make the batter. It is best not make this dessert too far in advance.

Cookware needed – 10-inch cast iron skillet.

## INGREDIENTS

1 tablespoon unsalted butter

1 cup whole milk

½ cup sugar

3 extra large eggs

1 teaspoon vanilla extract

½ cup all-purpose flour

zest of 1 lemon

pinch of salt

12 oz. fresh fruit, blueberries, plums, peaches or cherries

*optional – confectioner's sugar for topping*


## DIRECTIONS

Preheat the oven to 400° F.

Grease the cast iron skillet with butter.

To a blender add the milk, sugar, eggs and the vanilla extract. Blend for 20 seconds, or until the batter is smooth.

In a small bowl combine the flour, lemon zest and a pinch of salt.

Remove the blender cover and slowly add the flour mixture into the batter. Pulse gently until all the ingredients are fully incorporated.

Pour the batter into the cast iron skillet and arrange the fresh fruit on the top.

Bake for approximately 45 - 50 minutes, or until the cake sets and is a light golden brown color.

Remove from the oven and allow the skillet to cool for 15 minutes. While cooling the cake will deflate slightly.

*Optional* - dust with the confectioner's sugar.

Cut into wedges and, for the best results, serve warm.

# PHYLLO & FRUIT

An elegant dessert that tastes as fantastic as it looks.

## INGREDIENTS

8 sheets phyllo pastry dough

1 tablespoon unsalted butter, melted

1 tablespoon canola oil

8 oz. whipped cream cheese

3 tablespoons confectioner's sugar

1 cup heavy cream, whipped

16 oz. of fresh fruit, kiwi, strawberries, orange slices and blueberries

1 oz. white chocolate, melted

# <u>DIRECTIONS</u>

Preheat the oven to 400° F.

There are two ways to prepare this dessert. One is as the recipe describes or you may mold and shape the phyllo as shown. Finish with powdered sugar as desired.

Place the sheets of phyllo pastry on a smooth, dry surface. Cover with plastic film and then a slightly damp towel.

In a small bowl combine the melted butter and the oil.

Line a sheet pan with parchment paper.

Place one sheet of phyllo pastry on the parchment lined sheet pan. Evenly brush the sheet of phyllo with the butter/oil mixture. Add another sheet and again brush with butter/oil. Repeat until all the sheets of phyllo have been stacked on top of each other.

Place the phyllo pastry into the oven and bake for 5 - 7 minutes.

Remove the phyllo from the oven and cool on a wire rack.

In a small bowl beat together the cream cheese and the confectioner's sugar until smooth. Fold in the whipped cream. Gently spread over the cooled phyllo crust and arrange the fresh fruit on top.Drizzle the melted white choclate over the top in a nice crisscross pattern.

# Cassata Siciliana – Ricotta Sponge Cake with Liqueur & Candied Fruit

Traditionally an elaborate Italian cake made with marzipan (candied fruit). I have converted the traditional recipe into an easy to assemble cake.

## INGREDIENTS

1 10-inch sponge cake, store bought

3 tablespoons Grand Marnier (orange liqueur) or Marsala wine

2 lbs. fresh whole milk ricotta

2 cups powdered sugar

1 teaspoon vanilla extract

¼ teaspoon cinnamon

½ cup semi-sweet chocolate chips

1 cup candied fruit


## DIRECTIONS

Prepare the ricotta by wrapping in cheesecloth and nestling over a bowl in the refrigerator overnight. The excess moisture will be drained off by the morning. Drain and discard the liquid.

Place the ricotta into a bowl and using a mixer beat until the curds smooth out. Mix the ricotta with 1 cup of the powdered sugar, vanilla extract, cinnamon, chocolate chips until incorporated. Add ½ the candied fruit mixture. Stir then set aside.

Lightly spray a springform pan with canola oil.

Slice the sponge cake very thinly so that you can line the bottom and sides of the springform pan with even layers of the sponge cake. Reserve a final layer of the sponge cake for the top.

Line the bottom and sides of the springform pan with the sponge cake slices.

Brush the sponge with half the orange liqueur or Marsala wine.

Pour the ricotta filling into the sponge cake-lined springform pan and finish by laying the final piece of sponge cake on top.

Brush the top of the sponge with the remaining orange liqueur or Marsala wine.

Cover the cake with plastic wrap and refrigerate overnight.

When ready to serve invert the cake and release from the springform pan.

Top with the remaining powdered sugar and the remaining candied fruit.

Thinly slice the cake to serve.

# Portuguese Almond Tart - Tarte de Amêndoa Portuguesa

Bonus recipe by José Tavares – editor.

This is one of my favorite tarts. I first tasted this gloriously delicious tart when travelling in Portugal and had to try baking it myself. It is rich and nutty and a little goes a long way. It will easily serve 8 people.

I have included directions for making your own pastry dough if you have the time or are feeling adventurous. Using shop bought pie crust is also perfectly ok.

## INGREDIENTS

For the pastry

1 ¼ cups (5 ½ oz.) all-purpose flour

⅓ cup (2 ¾ oz.) salted butter

½ cup (2 ½ oz.) superfine sugar

1 large free-range egg yolk

*optional – 1 Pillsbury pie crust, thawed*

For the filling

2 ½ cups (8 oz.) flaked (sliced) almonds

4 ½ oz. salted butter

⅔ cup (4 ¼ oz.) superfine sugar

4 tablespoons whole milk

1 teaspoon vanilla paste or extract

*optional – ½ teaspoon almond extract*

*optional – confectioner's sugar for dusting*

## DIRECTIONS

Preheat the oven to 340° F.

For the pie crust.

Add the flour, butter and superfine sugar to a food processor and mix until it resembles breadcrumbs.

Add the egg yolk and 2 teaspoons of cold water and mix until the dough comes together. Roll out on a clean, floured surface to a thickness of just under ¼-inch and a little wider than the base of a 9½-inch fluted tart pan with a removable base.

*Optional* – To save time and effort use a Pillsbury pie crust instead of making your own.

Lay the pastry onto the base of the pan and use your fingers to press the pastry into the corners of the pan and about a ½ inch up the side, creating an even lip all around the sides.  Cover with plastic wrap (saran) and refrigerate for at least 30 minutes.

Remove the plastic wrap and prick the pastry base lightly all over with a fork. Line with baking paper and pour in baking beans or lentils. Bake for 15 minutes. Remove the baking beans and paper and return to the oven for 3 – 4 minutes to dry out the base, without coloring. Remove from the oven and set aside.

To make the filling.

Toast the almonds in a dry skillet pan over medium-high heat for 2 – 3 minutes, or until lightly golden-brown. Shake the pan occassionaly. Keep a close eye on the nuts so they do not over-brown or burn. Pour the nuts into a bowl.

Put the butter, superfine sugar and milk in the skillet over medium heat. When the superfine sugar has dissolved and the butter melted bring to the boil and boil for 1 minute. Add the almonds and mix well before pouring into the pie crust.

Bake for 15 – 20 minutes, or until the top is a rich golden-brown.

Remove from the oven and leave to cool on a wire rack.

Serve warm or cold. I prefer it at room temperature.

*Optional* – dust with confectioner's sugar if serving cold.

# FROM THE AUTHOR. THANK YOU!

# Thank
# You

Thank you very much for reading my book. If you love my recipes please tell you friends and family about my cookbook. A good review on Amazon would be greatly appreciated.

# MORE ABOUT THE AUTHOR.

Find out more about me and lots more wonderful recipes, tips and techniques by reading my blog.
www.positiveliving.solutions/

# OTHER BOOKS BY THIS AUTHOR

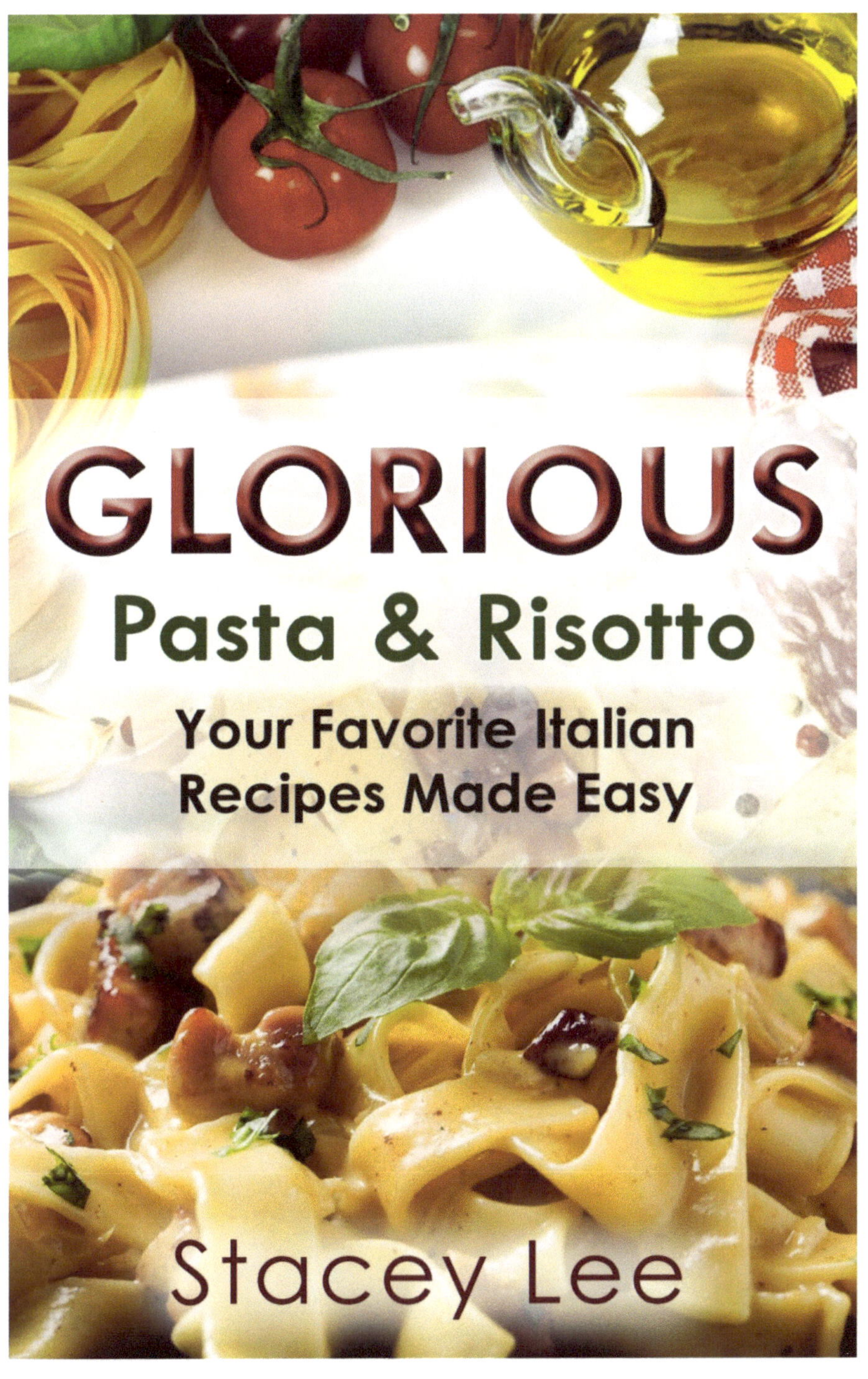